THE TWO PENNIES

A TRUE STORY FROM THE TITANIC

To Libby,

Susie Millar

I hope this is a good memory of
your Belfast visit,

Sue Millar

15.9.16.

Published by:
Susie Millar - Titanic Tours Belfast

www.titanictours.co

Design & layout by Gavin Moffitt

ISBN: 978-0-9571936-9-7

This book is also available in Kindle and iBooks format

ACKNOWLEDGEMENTS

I would like to thank my husband, Gavin, for putting up with my technical incapability and for his work on this new version of the book and the ebook versions.

Thanks also to my Mum, Lila and my sister, Fiona for their encouragement on all of my Titanic related projects.

Finally, to the artist, Debra Wenlock, a fellow Titanic enthusiast for doing such a lovely job of the original watercolour used on the front cover of this book.

April 2012

Chapter One:

Jeannie Ruddock - 1898

How I look forward to a day I can have completely to myself, a day to sit by the fire and think my own thoughts without anyone asking me what I am doing or why I am not helping with all that needs done around the house. Since Mother died, Maggie and I have taken on her role, kept this family on its feet. Father is still earning a fair enough wage even though he is 64 now and his eyesight is starting to give him trouble.

When you are a cabinet maker, that isn't the best thing to happen. The family decided we needed more money coming in to put bread on the table and of course it fell to Maggie and me to start taking in washing.

I am sure my father doesn't like the idea of his daughters slaving away for other people but at the same time it gives us girls a little money of our own to spend on ourselves. My oldest brother, Bob says there is no way we will get anyone to marry us at the best of times, let alone if our dresses look shabby. What he has failed to take notice of is the state of my poor hands which look like they belong to a 50 year old instead of a 20 year old.

The days are all much the same. Up at the skrake of dawn, boiling water on the stove, sheet upon shirt upon skirt upon petticoats into the tub and then the never ending scrub scrub scrub until they are clean. But do you know the part I hate the most? The folding of it all afterwards. That is a job for two people but Maggie is never to be found at the critical moment. Maggie loves to gossip. It is without doubt her favourite thing to do in all of her life, to stand in the street with the neighbours and gossip about whatever is new, who is doing what, yacking away to anyone who will stand still long enough to listen to her. When I read back what I have written here it makes me sound like a bitter old mare. I don't mind her doing what she wants but there is so much to do in the house with all these lazy men living here. Bob is a fine one to talk about us girls being left on the shelf when there isn't a woman to be seen between all my brothers.

I like my life despite the hard work and the teasing I get from the boys. I would say I have a sunny nature. I love to sing, to play the mouth organ and to have fun with my brothers. Life is not really so bad here. Our neighbours here in Trafalgar Street are good to us and we like to get together on a Saturday night and swap old stories.

When it comes time for the singing they always call on me first to do a turn. I am not shy about singing unlike some of the girls. What would be the point in hiding your light under a bushel? I know I have a good voice because if I didn't, folk round here wouldn't be long about letting me know it and telling me to sit back down again.

But they never do, they let me sing on and on so it must have some sort of melody to it. Some of the older ones I have even seen wipe a tear from their eye when I am in the middle of a sad song. Hugh says they are crying because my voice is so bad. My brothers all tease me and say I should put myself on the music hall stage.

They aren't so complimentary about the mouth organ though. They said last week I would do well in some dockside pub. I can brush that aside because I know they are just jealous because they have not one scrap of talent between the lot of them.

Then the banter will start up again about being 20 and no sign of a man to walk me to the end of the street never mind take me out to a dance or the far-fetched chance of someone wanting to walk me up the aisle. All of this never fails to stop amusing my brothers who never think that the reason I have no time to go gallivanting is that I am too busy looking after them.

And sure the men round here are so busy working and trying to impress each other with how tough they are, they have not the first idea of how to even talk to a woman let alone court her. Hugh, my youngest brother has just started work as a mechanic in York Street.

He likes his work, it would be a lot easier than the docks or the cigarette factory or the ships. The only thing is since he started working there, he is never done smoking. It must be the fellas he works along with have started him at that and now our Maggie is smoking too. Every time you look at Hugh he has a fag in his mouth, one after another. But there I go again, giving out about folk. You would never think I was a cheery soul underneath these aprons and rough washerwoman's hands.

Maybe I am old before my time living here in this wee kitchen house looking after everyone else's wants and needs, sleeping top to toe with my sister. Still, what else is there?

Chapter Two:

Tom Millar - 1898

It was not a hard decision to come home to Ireland. I missed the old place when I was away in Barrow. There were clear days when I could see across the sea to the coast of County Down and there were dark days when it might as well have been as far away as the Orient. I came back about four weeks ago now. All the ship work was coming to Belfast and I have followed it. If I am to get fully qualified as a shipwright I need to be working on the big projects and keep in steady work so when I got a letter from Harland and Wolff to say there was a chance to serve my time here, and become an engineer, I didn't have to think too long about my answer. It was the perfect opportunity to come back from England.

What I learned in Barrow and at the wee yard before that will always stand me in good stead. But Harland and Wolff? They are the big guns, the shipbuilders to the world, ambitious, expanding all the time. I need to be part of that. The few bits and pieces I had stored up with my family in Carrickfergus got sent down on a cart last week. I am not a great one for possessions but you need a few things to call your own when you are boarding.

My Uncle William is more like an older brother to me. When my parents died, he took me under his wing. He is already settled and married with a big brood of children. He is building his own house in Boneybefore, a wee village where us Millars have lived for what seems to be hundreds of years. It is only a tiny village of two or three streets but at one time, every other house had a Millar living in it.

William could never understand why I didn't just stay in the local yards up the coast and stay round home with the rest of the family. I could never explain to him that I wanted something with prospects, maybe something that will take me across the oceans eventually. My father was a sailor so I suppose that is where I get it from. Ireland is a fine place, friendlier than England that's for sure but you only get one crack at this life and I would like to see something of the world.

My father said if I thought like that I should have joined the forces but I want to make my own way on my own terms, not shining someone else's boots. So here I am, the wandering man back home, or 20 miles down the road from where I was born. The further and harder you try to get away, the stronger the pull to bring you back.

So I am boarding with a woman called Mrs Henry here in Trafalgar Street. It is a long narrow street which seems to be the main drag through Sailortown, so called because it is right next to the docks. I haven't got to know anyone yet, either in the street or at work but then I am not the chattiest over lunch or anything like that.

Last time I boarded here when I was at Workman's yard, I was only a pup, scared to talk to anyone. There were four of us boarding in the one house with Mrs Cairns. We would hang around together, even outside of work; we used to play cards for matches.

It was the foreman at Workman's who told me about the job at Vickers, across the water. I didn't have to be told twice. The other lads are all still at the wee yard doing much the same thing. A couple of them got work at the docks or at Gallagher's, all this side of the river you see. Some of them are too scared to go to the big yard on the far shore of the river let alone the adventures I have had the past few years. It is different for me and now I am one of the ferry boys who gets the wee boat across the channel to go to work in the North yard. Ferry would be too grand a term for it now. If you don't fight your way to the front and jump off before she has even touched land, you can easily find yourself back where you started at Clarendon Dock and late for work into the bargain. That's when the timekeeper starts docking your wages and there is no talking your way out of that. The trick is to grab your board from the timekeeper and get to where you are working before the "hat" comes round to check how hard you are working.

I am picking up all the rules as quickly as I can. You have to or you get left behind and nobody is going to hold your hand and tell you how it should be done. Not unless your father is working here and passes on all the shortcuts, but that wouldn't apply to me, would it? I just keep my eyes open to what the others are doing and try to do the same.

Enough of work now. I may be ambitious but I know there is a life outside work at the same time. There are plenty of other things in life and there is little point to having a good wage and money in your pocket for spending if there is no-one to enjoy it with. Living in a rented room in a boarding house is not how I want to end up.

Chapter Three:

William Millar - 1900

I can hardly believe it is the first year of the century. It is hard to imagine it is now the 1900's. I wonder will things be very different? Mary and I brought the new century in with the family, the older children were allowed to stay up until we could hear the boats out on the lough sounding their horns. My nephew, Thomas came up from Belfast for a few days to see us. We have hardly seen him at all since he moved back from England. He is working very hard down at the shipyard there. He was always more ambitious than me, never content to stand still for too long, always looking for the next bigger and better job. He always had more spark about him.

All I wanted to do was learn to build, plaster and that sort of thing, to work with my hands and create something people could live in. This little cottage has been in the family for years and I keep doing wee bits and pieces to it for Mary and the children. Nobody can even remember how the Millars came to be here in Boneybefore, there seems to have been a Millar here forever.

My late brother, Thomas says our ancestors came from Renfrew in Scotland and were soldiers and I have no reason to doubt him. I can't even really remember how we came upon this particular house but I see no reason to be anywhere else but here.

It makes a fine home for my brood. I am glad we were able to spend some time with Tom and hear how his life is going and to have him with us to welcome in the new century. Maybe now he will come and see us more often, now that he is settled in Harland's.

The children love to hear his tales of all the old cods he works with and the stories they tell. Our children think he is very exotic because he has lived across the water for a while. Imagine that, my wee nephew the traveller. Sure I used to look out for him when he was a wee skitter in bare feet and short trousers.

Now he is on the up. Who knows where he will end up from what he was saying to us. He picked the right trade to be involved with. Me and Mary are just the country cousins now.

Chapter Four:

Hugh Ruddock - 1900

I love having sisters. They are so easy to wind up and annoy. It provides me with hours of entertainment to see just how far I can push them before they crack up with me.

Our Maggie likes nothing better than to peak out the window and see what's going on in the street. Even when there is nothing at all going on in the street, there she will stand at the front window hoping for something to happen that she can then go and talk about to whoever will listen. So a couple of days ago, I crept out through the back yard and ran round to the front of the street.

She thinks I am still sitting in the kitchen listening to her talking on and on about something. I hid down below the level of the sill and when she was in the middle of staring into the distance, I jumped up from below and scared the wits clean out of her. It makes me laugh for hours just thinking about the look of shock on her face. Jeannie is the same, she sings away to herself when she thinks she is alone. Singing as she does the washing, in a world all of her own. She makes it so easy to sneak up behind her and grab her round the waist. That makes her jump out of her skin. Both the girls have threatened that they will stop making me any lunch to take to work with me if I continue to torment them but I know there is no chance of that happening.

Our Jeannie is a soft touch. She needs to watch herself though or she will end up being left on the shelf. Try telling her that and she gives you a clip round the ear. She treats me like I am younger than her, not older but then she says I act like a child and she will treat me like an older brother when I start acting like one. Annie, the only one of my sisters who has managed to get herself a man and keep him, she is never done trying to fix Jeannie up with some man or other but with no success. Jeannie just says she doesn't like the look of them.

So last Friday I was walking back from work and I fell into stride with another fella who was going the same way up our street. We got to talking like you do because you can't walk in silence with a person beside you and he told me he was serving his time at the yard. Now this boy looked about 20 so I asked him how come he was only doing his apprenticeship at that age. He said he had started over again because he wanted to do it right, learn all about the technical bits of how to build the engines for ships and how they worked.

He is a carpenter now, learning all about joinery and how to build wooden gantries and props for underneath the ships. Not only does he have to work all day but some nights he has to study up on other stuff. Work is hard enough without stretching it into your evening as well I told him but he just laughed that off.

Anyway this fella, Tom you call him, we got on pretty well so I asked Da about inviting him in to one of the gatherings we have in the house for some of the neighbours on a Saturday.

These lads who board with Mrs Henry up the street, they have a lonely enough time of it if they don't know anyone in the city. I am sure no-one will object to a new face in our kitchen at the weekend. Heaven knows it can get tedious enough with the same old folk week in week out, same old stories, same old songs. Maybe this fella will have something new to add to the mix.

Chapter Five:

Tom Millar - 1900

This young man I met in the street the other day, he called to Mrs Henry's door last Friday and asked me if I wanted to come to one of the neighbours houses the following night for a bit of a get together. Just a fireside gathering to make a difference between the working week and time off. To be honest with you I didn't think they went in for that sort of thing up here in the city but this end of town seems quite friendly.

Back in Carrickfergus we were in and out of the neighbours' houses all the time but people here in the city keep much more to themselves so it was pleasant to be invited in. I am not much of a one for singing but I can listen and I can spin out a tale if I am forced into it. I thought about it and since the only people I get to talk to these days are people telling me what to do I thought I might stick my head in for half an hour since the weather was cold and Mrs Henry, good though she is, doesn't believe in keeping a roaring fire in the grate.

There were about twenty people in the wee kitchen house, not enough seats for everyone but that's good because you can hide by the door and make your escape if you find it isn't your scene. Your man Hugh who invited me in the first place, he has a big family, three sisters and three brothers.

His father is the head of the house but he is a quiet old man. There were others there as well who I was introduced to you but to be honest I cannot remember who was who. I recognised a few of the older ones from living on this street.

Although I had my doubts at first, now I am glad that I went and there is one good reason for that.

This girl, Jeannie her name was. Brown eyes, long wavy brown hair, the tiniest nipped-in wee waist I have ever seen. She smiled over at me a couple of times and later she handed me a cup of tea. But it was when she started to sing that she really got my attention. She sang a song called "silver bell". She had to be asked three times to take the floor but it wasn't false modesty, just a little shyness I think because until she got into her stride in the second verse, her face was the colour of a riveter's thumb.

When she finished her brother, Samuel persuaded her to give us all a tune on her French fiddle. At that some of her family began to dance a bit of a jig and I got the feeling her brothers were taking a hand out of her like it was some private family joke but she gave them such a look that they soon sat down and she played on.

I caught her eye again when she had finished and sat back down in her chair. She smiled at me. That was it, just a smile. Goodness knows I have not even exchanged a word with the woman apart from a thank you for the cup of tea but I can't stop thinking about her and her lovely soft singing voice.

Chapter Six:

Jeannie Ruddock - 1900

I had a feeling our William and Hugh were up to something over the last few days and it quickly became clear when a stranger came along with my brother to the wee gathering we have some Saturday nights. Thomas was how he introduced himself. Average height, fair hair, pale blue eyes, workman's hands. I always notice the hands because there is no point tying yourself up with some layabout that wouldn't know a good day's work if it hit him up the face. Shy, he was.

He didn't take a turn at entertaining but then you would not expect someone who had just walked through the door to a room full of strangers to put himself forward so that is all right. In fact if he had come in and taken over the place I wouldn't have much time for him. If he had been forced to give us a song, the poor man might never have come back near any of us again and that would have been a shame. He smiled over at me a couple of times but I never got to talk to him. Maybe he will come back again. It will be our turn again in a few weeks to have everyone over to our house.

For some reason, I really do hope he comes. He seems a little more mature than my brothers, even our Bob who is fifteen years older than me and thinks he knows all there is to know about everything. Bob works as a joiner in the yard but before that he was at sea for a while. Whatever happened, it didn't work out for him because he came back after a couple of years. Life at sea must not have suited him.

William works in a rent agent's office and he says he can get us a better deal on a place in Meadow Street. He said something about me and Maggie being permanent fixtures so since nobody is planning on moving out and getting a home of their own any time soon, he should look about getting us a bigger house. It would be a shame to leave Trafalgar Street. We were all born in this house and Ma died here. Maybe that memory of her has lingered too long and it is time to move on. Da is talking about retiring finally so it might be a good idea to let him live out his days in a place that is not a constant reminder of his poor wife.

Do you know what Da said to me the other day? He said, "I can't be retiring, I am an artisan." In the name of heavens, where did he pick that up from? The idea! Where can he have heard that?

That's one thing about the Ruddocks. They can always be relied upon to come up with ideas above their station.

Chapter Seven:

Tom Millar - 1900

It was no use really. I had to go ahead and do it. Jeannie Ruddock would not leave my head alone. From that first time I saw her and heard her sing I knew there would be no other girl for me. Now I am not a great man for romance. Heaven knows if any of the lads at work knew I had gone soft over a lass, they would have taken the hand out of me.

But a man has to settle down eventually and if I am going to make my home in Belfast and stick with Harland's then I should be doing it sooner rather than later. We haven't enough for a home of our own yet but we can sort something out until I get into the really skilled work.

So I asked her, last night. Even though we have only known each other about six months now, mostly just talking or going out for walks, I can't see me getting a better person to get along with. She belongs to the Church of Ireland on Donegall Street, the big one although Jeannie says they only ever use the side chapel. The rector there says he will marry us in a few months.

I asked William if he will be my best man, if he will get the train down from Boneybefore but he is so busy with building and the children so I suppose not. Out of Jeannie's four brothers, Hugh is the one I get on with best. He is the closest to my age and I think he understands about seeing other places and the idea that there is a big world beyond Belfast. He is a mechanic and he wants to go somewhere like Canada to live.

Robert, Jeannie's older brother is the quiet one. He was away at sea for a short while but he didn't take to it. I don't know why as he is not the type to discuss it. Now he works as a joiner, same as his father did. He has been working on some of the ships at the wee yard. I told him there was more plentiful work at Harland's but I can't start telling somebody far older than me what he should be doing with himself so I haven't pushed it.

Samuel and William the other brothers haven't managed to find themselves anyone to marry either. Sometimes I reckon they have it too easy with Maggie and Jeannie to look after them, send them out in the morning with a piece of bread for their lunch and have their tea ready when they get in the door from work.

Then there is Hugh, my friend who hasn't a serious bone in his body. He just acts the lig the entire time. I can't see anyone taking him on and I have told him as much. I suppose the boys will think I am taking Jeannie away from them, that there will be one less pair of hands to keep house for them but I would say we will be in with the rest of them in Meadow Street for a few years yet until I get some money saved up for our own place.

And Maggie the dreamer couldn't cope on her own with five men to look after. Jeannie's married sister, Annie is married to a fella called John Boyd and they have a small family of their own. Even though they are only a few streets away they don't bother so much with the rest of the family.

Speaking of which, I haven't seen my own lot for months now, since the start of the year.

My youngest cousin, Andrew is a bright wee thing. Last time I was down there I gave him a little wooden man I had carved with my penknife one lunch break. His mother says he loves that thing better than any of his other toys, all passed down through the six other children before they reach him. Maybe that's why it is special to him because it is the only thing that only belongs to him. I like to sit and carve figures at lunch break, it beats losing money at cards or going to one of those religious meetings, that's for sure.

Things are starting to get much busier at the Yard. You can see it everywhere you look. There are more people about, more supplies coming through the sheds, all the slipways busy. The older ones say that since Pirrie took over, the orders have got more and more and the ships themselves more complicated and ambitious. Adriatic and now the Oceanic that we are building for White Star are the biggest things I have ever seen, none of your old wooden tubs that I was working on in Barrow.

It is all big heavy steel steamers these days. The foreman signed me up for classes at the technical college in the centre of town, a big imposing building. I felt like a fraud going in there with all these people in their best suits but if that is where I have to go to learn, then so be it. Some of the week I learn technical drawing, other days its engineering, how things work, how you turn all that steam from the boilers into power to turn the engines.

Who thinks up these processes? Who is it that sits down with a piece of paper and works out how it all adds up? If I could learn about engines and how they work, that sort of knowledge could take Jeannie and me anywhere in the world that we wanted to go.

Chapter Eight:

Jeannie Ruddock - 1900

When I told Maggie first that I was getting married to Tom, she looked a bit upset. I suppose she thought that with my being the baby of the family, I should wait for her to get hitched first but she has never made any progress in that direction. Tom and I get on so well that there didn't seem to be any point in waiting.

So we had a quiet wedding service at St Paul's church and then back here for a bit of a gathering. Tom's uncle didn't make it down from the country in the end. He thought he would but as it turned out the weather was so bad that the roads were all churned up with mud and he couldn't even get out of Carrickfergus let alone down the road to Belfast.

I suppose it is a bit far to travel when he has a lot of work on, so in the end there was nobody there from Tom's family at all. If he was annoyed he didn't show it. He has always been so independent and all he said on the matter was that we were his family now and that is good enough for him. Just as well he likes us since we are all squeezed into this tiny house in Meadow Street living on top of each other.

If I thought I had no privacy at the last place, then this is even worse. Still, the best thing to come out of it as far as Maggie is concerned is that there is no more washing to take in. Tom said since his wage was going into the family pot, there was no need for us to be doing other people's work. That brought a smile to Maggie's face all right.

If she had doubts about Tom before, he soon won her round with that statement.

Don't be fooled, there is still plenty of work to do around the house but at least it is within the family and nothing to do with other folk.

Just as well Tom made that decision about the washing because there will be another little Millar mouth to feed early next year.

Chapter Nine:

Hugh Ruddock - 1900

Another year started and still not a Ruddock man married off yet. Sometimes I think my brothers and I have something in our character that must be repellent to women because not one of them seems to want to know us.

Bob showed a bit of an interest in a lassie from church, Agnes her name was but he probably bored the living daylights out of her and she took off as fast as her legs would carry her when his intentions were made known. I know I didn't help matters by telling Agnes that our Bob was as tight with his wages as any man she would ever run across.

Maybe that was what scuppered it because she high tailed it after that. The laugh of it is Bob is very generous about his money and I don't think he is speaking to me now. I reckon if she was that easily put off, she can't have been too interested in the whole thing to begin with.

Anyway, our Jeannie had a son at the start of February and she and Tom decided on the highly original name of Thomas. What is it with folk and carrying on family names? Can they not think of something different?

If you call out for William in our house, a squad of people will shout back, "What?"

Why not call him something that nobody else in the street is called let alone somebody else in the same house?

That comment got me the usual clip round the ear from Maggie the Maid. There are too many people living in this house, all with their own opinions.

Chapter Ten:

Tom Millar - 1901

Thomas Millar junior is six months old now. Actually, if you count my father, he is Thomas Millar the third. I wonder if he will have a son called Thomas some day in the future?

Sometimes I can't get over how quickly life has changed since I came back, how so much has been added to my life. It is all to the good of course.

I am putting away as much money as I can each week so that Jeannie and I can get ourselves a proper home. I have spoken to William about some of the houses in Spamount Street that we could maybe rent so possibly by the end of the year we could have our own front door.

To be honest, I don't think her old man has long left. Maggie will take it very badly because she is very close to her father but maybe when he is gone it will give her the freedom to live her own life. She spends most of her day looking after him, making him cups of tea and making sure he is warm by the fire.

Chapter Eleven:

Jeannie Millar - 1906

I think this house has been unlucky for us. Since we moved here after Thomas was born, Tom's work has been strange. Tom wants to get on in life, to get to the top of his profession and become an engineer. But the yard has kept him on carpenter's wages until a space comes up in the engine works. He is frustrated, and rightly so.

Jobs have come up but they always go to the sons of fathers who are retiring or moving on somewhere else. That can't be fair when he spends so much time studying about engines and the like.

And for me it has been a strange time as well these past few years. As soon as Thomas was walking, I knew it was time to add to the family and I wanted to have more, a big family like I come from but it didn't happen.

Time after time I lost them, until this time. I keep hoping against hope that this time I can carry the child to the end. I think I am safe now and Sarah who lives down the street and has delivered hundreds of children she says the only way to make it happen is not to worry about it.

Just three more months to wait and hope. Tom says I have to put my feet up and rest but that is a hard thing to do when there are so many tasks to be getting on with.

I have to get him out to work first thing in the morning, get the fire on and make Thomas his breakfast.

Then there is washing and cleaning to be done. The neighbours would be talking about you if your step wasn't washed down and sparkling clean. I cannot see how it makes a hoot of difference but I don't like to be talked about.

The other day I was singing a little song to myself, well actually not to myself, I was singing it out loud if I am honest. Well the woman across the road was out doing something much the same and I swear, she tutted at me, as if signing a song was some sort of crime.

It can't have been that offensive to her ears to have one of her neighbours sing as she scrubs her step. It is clear to me that nobody ever told that woman it is good to start the day with a song. Besides, my step is as clean as any in this street.

Tom is still carving away at his little wooden figures. There are dozens of them hidden all around the house for Thomas to find. He hides them under Thomas's pillow, even in the sugar bowl so that when I got to put sugar in the wee lad's tea, there is a little wooden creature lying against the spoon.

"How did it get there?" the bewildered child will ask me.

"The fairies must have put it there," is the only explanation I can ever come up with and that seems to satisfy him for now.

So now I have a five year old child who firmly believes that fairies are hiding little wooden men around the house for his amusement.

Chapter Twelve:

Tom Millar - 1907

Hugh laughed when he heard what we are calling the wee one. William, after both of our fathers and two of our brothers, and then Ruddock for Jeannie's family.

Except the man from the corporation who was registering the birth and giving us the certificate took the name down wrong, spelt it with an i instead of a o. So he's Ruddick instead of Ruddock.

Now that she has got over the annoyance, Jeannie quite likes it. He was supposed to go by William but he ends up getting called Ruddick to avoid confusion, or a mixture of both. I am glad it is another boy. His older brother can look out for him and anyway, it is no life being a woman in this day and age. All you end up doing is cleaning and cooking while the men make all the decisions. That's what Jeannie tells me, anyway.

I'd say that is our little family complete now. I know Jeannie would like more but it isn't worth the heartache you go through when she loses them, let alone the physical pain. Two is plenty. Sure look at my uncle, William's lot still living in that tiny cottage in Boneybefore. Eight children and two adults. Where they all put themselves I have no idea.

Things are much better for me at work now. The yard is really flourishing.

Last year they redesigned the whole North end of the works to put in new slipways. The idea was that they could take more weight and we could start to build heavier ships. They had to dredge out the channels too.

The rumour is that the big bosses have secured a huge order from White Star. Down at the far end, about a mile away from where I work, they are digging out a new dry dock big enough to take ships nine hundred feet long. It is where they will finish off these big creatures. I wouldn't be down that end of the yard ever but the gaffer took me down there to have a look a couple of weeks ago and the length of it? Whatever type of ships they have in mind to fill it should keep a lot of men in work for years to come.

I can't even imagine the type of thing they have in mind that would need so big a dock to hold them. The problem has been though that when they were hollowing out all that earth, the other dock started to collapse in on itself because there was nothing to hold it up. They have lost months of work because of that.

As for me, I am in the engine sheds way up at the other end. By day I am on the production line, working on the plans for how the ship's engines are going to fit together. Then it's off to classes to learn more about the trade. It is all to do with steam pressure, expansion of water when it heats and pounds per square inch.

I am learning about the heart of an engine, what makes it go, how you make it go faster and get the best from all the components. I would never have seen myself as a scholar but I love learning new things about the latest discoveries.

Who would have thought a country bumpkin like me would be on the front line of all this innovation, grasping the whys and wherefores of engineering and physics?

Still, I love it. I wouldn't have it any other way and the more examinations I pass, the more coins there are in the wage envelope at the end of the week.

The gaffer wants me to go for marine engineer qualifications. He says I am smart enough to get them. It is good to have that encouragement and recognition after years of being passed over for other people's sons. That is how it works in here, always has and probably always will.

I am happy with my home life too. After Jeannie's Da died, things went a bit sombre. Some of the boys moved in with Annie and her family because Maggie threw the head up and said she was fed up to the back teeth looking after four big lazy lumps and it was time they made their own way. Jeannie says she can see Maggie's point of view.

Anyway to try to keep the peace and to get the family back on course again, Jeannie decided to start doing Saturday night gatherings again, the way the Ruddocks used to do in Trafalgar Street when Jeannie and I first met. All of them except for Bob have been round to us. Samuel is away working near Dublin and seems to have settled well.

We have a bit of a sing song, the usual thing. I know the girls miss their father because I caught Maggie staring at the place where he used to sit. Some of the neighbours come in to us and it is good to catch up with what is going on in their lives.

After working so hard all week, the Saturday gathering is a good way to relax.

Though I love my work, there are some mornings I could just roll over and go back to sleep rather than dragging myself out into the cold air and following behind hundreds of other men on the trudge to the yard.

Saturday evenings, with a bit of banter and entertainment are something to look forward to. Sometimes the men even have a nip of whiskey on a special occasion.

Chapter Thirteen:

Jeannie Millar - 1908

I can't believe Tom has talked me into moving house again. It's not like we will notice much difference. After all, the new house is only two streets away from where we were but Tom says there is a world of a difference.

Hillman Street has parlour houses, he says and a man with a trade and a profession should live in a parlour house. He reminds me of the way my Da used to talk when he said he was an artisan. I don't mean any harm.

I am very proud of Tom and all the studying he has done to get to where he is. Tom is very ambitious and that can only be good for our family. With two young boys to think of we have to give them every chance for the future. If that future isn't here in Belfast then so be it. Everyone knows it is a tough life and you don't get handed anything for nothing. You have to make it happen for yourself. That's Tom's end of the bargain. He goes out and works and improves his skills. My part is to keep home, make sure he and the boys have everything they need and to make sure he takes some time off every now and then to spend with his family.

Last summer we would go to Alexandra Park on Sundays with the children. Tommy was off playing and wee Ruddick was lying on the blanket. Tom lies back and starts dreaming about all the places in the world those big ships are sailing to. He says the Yard is getting ready to build the biggest ships ever. They will be taller than all the mills in the city.

They are going to be sailing to America, taking lots of rich folk. Tom is going to be working on the engines of these new ships putting all the pieces together and fitting them on board the ships.

I don't know too much about all of that. I don't need to. I just know that when Tom starts to talk about his work, his face is shining with pride. I can't remember a time when he has been so happy and so involved in a project.

Me, I have to be content with my new parlour, which I was never really looking for in the first place. What on earth am I ever going to do with a parlour?

Annie says it is a room where you are supposed to sit around sipping tea out of china cups and talking about art and books. I can't see our Hugh lasting long in that environment. The other night on a Saturday I had a few of them round to see my parlour. Annie and John and Maggie. Bob and William came too for a while to pass themselves but let me tell you there was little talk about art and books. I doubt any of us has ever read a book the whole way through. Who would have the time?

I wanted our Saturday nights to be like the old days in Trafalgar Street when we used to have a bit of fun. It was enjoyable to a certain extent but I don't think any of my lot felt relaxed.

Something was missing. We didn't feel like a family any more. I suppose time moves on and there is nothing you can do about that but if there was a way to keep the family as close as we always were then I would try to make that happen.

Tom has lost touch with all of his brothers and sisters. I have two children to think of and they come first. I can't help thinking of the happy home we had when my mother was alive and how she kept us all together as best she could. I don't want us all to go off in our different directions when we live so close by to each other. Bob looks as if he is staying down South now but apart from him we are all living on each other's doorsteps so there is no reason why we all can't be as close as we once were.

At the end of the day it isn't up to me to put all the effort in. Keeping Tom and the boys is my first priority, not listening to William's tales of woe at work or how Hugh has failed in his latest attempt to get a girl to go with him. Anyway I won't give up on the rest of them.

They know the door is always open in Hillman Street any time they want to come round and visit. Even if the boys do tease me about my parlour house. A long way from taking in other people's washing, eh?

Chapter Fourteen:

Tom Millar (Aged 7) - 1908

When my wee brother was born, I was not happy about the situation. For so long it had been just me, Ma and Da although Da worked a lot and wasn't here much. Then suddenly there was this other person in the house with us, always wanting something, always crying.

Now that he is a bit older he is not just as noisy but he still gets a lot more attention from Ma. Ma calls him her wee blondie boy. He gets all the treats and smiles from my aunts and uncles. It's not me anymore. Now Da has started to make wooden men for him as well. It used to be just me that got toys made for me by Da.

I like going to school and learning my lessons. Ma will ask me all about what I have learned when I get back after lunchtime.

Once I have told her, I am allowed to go and play out on the street for a wee while.

Sometimes when I am out playing near the front door I can hear Ma coughing inside. She thinks I can't hear her but I can.

Once I asked her what was wrong but she just made a joke of it and told me go to and play.

Chapter Fifteen:

Tom Millar - 1910

A letter came last week. We don't get many letters to the house so it was a bit of a novelty all right. Unfortunately as is the case with most letters, it didn't bring good news.

My dear uncle, William in Carrickfergus, the one with all the children, he died about ten days ago. He was working on the roof of a house on the promenade in Whitehead, the next town over and something must have gone wrong because he just fell.

The man that was with him said he didn't lose his footing or anything like that. One minute he was working away, the next he just stopped like he had taken some sort of seizure. They got him onto a cart and brought him home to the cottage in Boneybefore. When the doctor was called, he said there was nothing he could do. He wasn't a young man, but he wasn't ancient either, just 58.

That leaves Mary with eight of them to bring up. Harry, her eldest is out working but the rest of them are a handful. I went up there on the train a few days ago.

Jeannie was going to come with me but she wasn't feeling well in the end. That's not like Jeannie to feel ill.

Anyway, William is buried in Victoria cemetery about a mile away from the village. Would you believe he bought a big plot there three years ago for the family? I wonder what he was thinking when he decided to do that. He was my closest relative because the two of us got on well.

Our family is not like Jeannie and her family where they see each other all the time and I feel now that he is gone that I never made the effort to get to know him properly.

He was that bit older than me but he was always interested in what I was doing.

It was a big funeral they had for him and all the people from his Orange lodge were there. They put his sash and the lodge banner over the coffin..

I know it sounds like an excuse for not seeing more of him but things at work are so busy and at the end of the day you are just glad to get sat down and some dinner rather than making plans to go and see relatives in the country.

I have been put on the engine squads for 401, the Titanic it is going to be called. Her sister, the Olympic is already well up off the ground. She will be launched soon. They have been painting her hull underneath the gantry these past few weeks so that she will look better when they take photographs of her. It is a shame I am not working on the Olympic's engines. She is the one everyone will be talking about. Who will remember the second ship in the class? Absolutely nobody! All the attention will be get focussed on the first ship, the biggest ever built.

Poor 401 will be the second fiddle. Of course, that's not what I tell the lads who are working on 400 of course. The ones in my squad put a brave face on it and tell the Olympic ones their ship will be out of date before it even sails but we all know that isn't true.

It's funny because watching 401 getting bigger and bigger

has got me thinking again about all the people and places she will see during her lifetime.

Jeannie knows what I think about all the opportunities that are out there. I have nearly all my qualifications finished now and those could take us anywhere in the world. Canada, America, wherever. People round here can't see past the end of the street let alone outside Belfast or Ireland.

I keep saying to Jeannie how great it would be to bring up the boys in a new young country where they can become whatever they want. I know Jeannie wants to be close to her family but to me, William's death just shows how short life is and we should make the most of every opportunity.

Every day I spend in the engine works building the mechanics to make these big ocean liners go, I spend some of that day thinking about the seas they will cross, the shores they will reach and I want a part of that for our little family.

It's a notion I have that won't seem to go away. I know I have a good career here with Harland's and the longer I spend here the higher I will go but I still believe there is more to life than the city of Belfast. I don't want to look back when I am 50 and say I should have done that, I should have looked for opportunities in other countries.

I should at least try to give it a go and if it doesn't work out, there is nothing much lost. I suppose I should be content for now. There are lots of people in this city who have no job at all let alone a good house, steady work and a family.

Chapter Sixteen:

Mary Millar - 1911

One thing is for sure, I will never be lonely even with William gone. Our house here could never be described as quiet. Since William died, the older children have been pulling their weight to make sure there is money coming in.

My girls are clever. They could all get good jobs if they want. We have all lived under the roof of this wee cottage for so long I can't imagine ever leaving it now. And the wee ones, Andrew and Ella, they love being next to the sea and watching the trains going past. Ella stands for hours on end and waves at the engine drivers as they pass by. She must look to them like some little waif standing by the trackside.

My eldest, Harry has bought himself the old tumbledown across the road. He says he is going to fix it up for him and Sarah. That way when he moves out he will only be a few steps away from his old Ma.

Meg has taken to sleeping in my room now to make more space for the others up in the rafters. Harry says he will fix up the thatch next Spring to make it cosier.

It is hard to look forward and plan for the future when I feel like this but what choice do I have when there is so much to be done in each day.

Chapter Seventeen:

Jeannie Millar - 1911

Tom was so excited when he got back today. The big ship he has been doing the engines for, they launched it at lunchtime. The noise was so loud I could hear it creaking and the chains clanking as she came off the big slipway and into the water. Tom says I imagined it but I swear Maggie and I heard the splash when the big boat hit the water. Tom says there is no way I would have heard that from back here but I swear I did.

Maybe I have been hearing so much about this big ship Titanic that I just thought I heard it. Maybe I just wanted to share in his excitement. The yard came to a standstill he says to watch the launch. They were allowed out of the works for half an hour to watch but of course that will come out of their pay at the end of the week. Tom says all the great and the good from White Star, the owners of the ship, were there to watch.

When it was all over, they got on with their work while the big wigs got on board Olympic and sailed over to Liverpool to show off their handiwork. The boys and I watched Olympic sail down Belfast Lough.

It will be funny to not see her sitting down at the wharf any more. We have all got used to these two big ships towering above everything else. Now there is just one.

Tom says some of the men get sad when a ship is launched because they are never sure whether there will be more work to replace it. There are always worries about people being let go.

But the word is that these two big ships will make Harland's so famous that everyone will want their big boats built there and there will be more than enough work for anyone who wants to work there. I didn't tell Tom that I was so tired in the middle of the day that I had to take myself off to bed. I fell asleep for over an hour until Tommy got back from school. I cannot figure out for the life of me why I feel so tired all of the time. Anyway this launch today has got Tom talking again about leaving here and seeing what opportunities there are in other countries.

Tom has always been the one to fly the nest. He says Belfast is such a small place and there are bound to be fortunes waiting to be made in other ports for men like him with experience on the big ships. I don't disagree with that but at the same time our home is here. We have got our families and they are a big part of the boys' lives.

If we go to somewhere like America we wouldn't know a soul. Who would look after Tommy and Ruddick if anything were to happen to us? Tom's work is likely to take him away and out of the house for hours if not days at a time. That would leave me stuck in a strange city where I know nobody and with no-one to talk to except the children. I suppose I am lucky I don't have one of those husbands who just decides how it is going to be and expects everyone else to go along with it without a word of discussion.

Tom is a good man and he knows if we are going to make a big step like he has in his mind, it needs to be everybody's choice or else it is not going to work. I know many a man who would just come home and lay down the law about how it is going to be. They bring home the money so they decide how it will be spent and how things will run. I couldn't have lived with a man like that.

It is probably why I picked Tom in the first place, because I knew he was good natured and considerate. He has a gentle side to him that I can work with. Not that I would use that to my advantage. And I certainly wouldn't say he is a soft touch. But we are much more of a partnership than any of the other marriages I know of.

Still, he won't let the idea go of uprooting to the other side of the world. Building these big ships has got him wondering about the places they will visit and I can understand that. There is life beyond Hillman Street that is for sure.

The big question is, is that a life that would suit us or that we would want to live?

Chapter Eighteen:

Ruddick Millar (Aged 4) - 1911

Da had been talking and talking about taking me and my brother out for a big surprise, for a big day out that we would enjoy but he wouldn't tell us until we got there what we were going to see. He said it was to happen on the next Sunday when it was fair.

Tommy tried and tried to make him tell us what the surprise was but he wasn't for telling. Then on Sunday morning he told us he was taking us to the place where he worked. I was frightened for a while because I thought he meant we would have to help him build engines like he does. I don't know how to do that. I can do my numbers and my words but I don't know how to hold a hammer or any of the other tools that Da uses.

I supposed he would teach us what we were to do when we got there. I didn't want to go into the noisy big shed where Da works because he had told us it is always full of people and you have to have your wits about you or you could get hit by something which would knock you off your feet.

But it turned out we weren't going to help him with his work after all. We were going to see a big boat. Da had been helping to make the engine for this boat that would make it go through the water. All the way down I was really excited.

Ma was supposed to come too but in the end she said she wanted a few hours to herself, a bit of peace and quiet in the house she said. I think Da was a bit upset that she didn't want to come and see his boat. He tried to get her to change her mind but she was having none of it.

"Take the boys," she said. "I will wait for you here and you can tell me all about it when you get back." Uncle Robert came instead. He is my Ma's brother and a long time ago he was a sailor. Ma dressed me up in my best clothes, a velvet suit with a sailor's collar and a velvet hat. Uncle Bob said I looked like a miniature version of him. I didn't want to wear the suit but Ma said what would happen if one of the important people from the yard was to see us? She said she didn't want them thinking she was bringing up urchins.

So all the way down I walked between Da and Uncle Robert until we got to the place where the big boat was sitting.. Da says it was called a wharf and he showed me a huge big crane which was there to lift heavy things onto the top of the boat.

There was a thing like a bridge as well so that all the people working on the boat could climb on board. Both of these things impressed me but for the life of me I couldn't see what he meant when he was talking about the ship.

"Look, Rud," he said. "That big thing there, that's the big ship I have been telling you about. It's all the one thing. That's the Titanic. Imagine all the fine ladies and gentlemen who will be passengers on this when it sails to America in a few months."

I looked and looked but I couldn't see what he was talking about. He couldn't mean this big metal mountain that was in front of me. It looked to me like a street of towering, frightening buildings. That wasn't a boat. A boat was something you could see all at once, with a chimney and a rudder and an anchor. This was just a big mass blocking out the light and filling the horizon. Sure you couldn't even see the Cavehill behind it.

Da must have seen that I looked confused because he pointed at it again. "That's the Titanic there," he said. "That big object, the biggest that man has ever built. And built by us here in the yard in wee Belfast. People will talk about this ship for years to come," he said. And with that he started to tell Uncle Bob all about how the engines worked, how many there were and how fast she could go. I didn't understand all what he was saying and I think Uncle Robert was not really following him either but he kept nodding his head as if he did. I didn't want Da to know that I was disappointed by his big surprise that was our treat for the day so I smiled a lot and pretended to be happy but the big boat frightened me.

I don't know what my brother thought about it all because he didn't say much.

Tommy never says too much about anything. He will answer your question if you ask him but that is about the end of it. He will never offer you any extra information aside from what you ask him. He is six years older than me and Ma says when I appeared in the house Tommy was jealous because he didn't get all the attention any more.

He will speak to me sometimes if he thinks I am in trouble or someone isn't playing fairly in the street but that is about all. Otherwise I am just his annoying little brother.

Anyway we all went home, Uncle Robert and me telling Da it was the greatest thing we had ever seen. Later on I heard the grown-ups talking downstairs.

Uncle Robert was telling Da he didn't see how the big boat was ever going to be able to move. "She's too big," he said, "far too big. How is she ever going to move? It isn't right to build a ship that size. You can't manage them. You never know what will happen."

"Nonsense," Da said. "She's as safe as houses. In fact they say it's nearly impossible to sink her."

Chapter Nineteen:

Tom Millar - Late 1911

A few days ago the gaffer told me something and I can't shake it from my mind. No matter how hard I try.

He told me White Star, the crowd who own and run the ships we are building, well they are looking for engineers to go to sea with these big ships, people who know the inner workings of them. They say they haven't enough people to man the ships out at sea right now, and that's before Titanic starts operating. He told me the head man was here in Belfast and he wanted to talk to people who were interested, trained engineers. It would be perfect for me.

All right, it means I would have to leave Jeannie and the boys for stretches at a time but it means I could get to see other parts of the world and maybe get an idea what it would be like to live there, see where would suit us. I could work for White Star over on the other side. It might take me a wee while to get us somewhere to live, find a nice neighbourhood where the boys can grow up but it would be worth it in the long run to give them a better future.

My wages here are fair enough, but the ones White Star are paying would be double that.

Think of all the things I could buy for Jeannie with all that extra money coming in.

So today I tracked down this man. I went after work to see him at the Grand Central hotel. I asked the man at the desk if I could speak to him.

I have to admit I was a bit nervous turning up out of the blue but if the man was here to find people interested in work, there would be little point in letting him leave town without putting my name forward.

As it turned out, he was a decent fella. He asked me a few questions about my job and why I would want to be a sea going engineer when I had a perfectly good job here on land. He said I would have to be away from shore for long periods of time and that the work would be tough. It would be about trouble-shooting, finding problems before they became problems and sorting them out, using my own initiative a lot of the time. He gave me the address of a man in Liverpool that I was to write to, setting out all my qualifications and the like and what sort of wage I wanted to get paid. Imagine, me telling them what I should get paid rather than the other way round!

The man said if they like the sound of me, I could be a White Star engineer by the start of next year, once they give me a bit of training.

So then I came home and told Jeannie. She wondered what was keeping me so long getting up the road home because I never dawdle or go for a drink like some of the others. I knew Jeannie might not be too happy that I had gone ahead and enquired. I know she doesn't really understand why I should give up a decent life here to go careering round the world.

Tommy is settled in school and we have all our family round us. That would be more than enough for most people. The only thing that is out of place with our wee life at the moment is that Jeannie looks so tired these days.

You would seldom hear her singing any more or playing the mouth organ for the boys.

Maybe she is just worn out with the children to look after but the other day when she was bringing in coal from the yard, it was like it took nearly all the energy she had just to do that one thing. She had to stop for a rest half way back to the door.

She didn't realise I had been watching her and she never mentioned it so I decided not to say anything either, but it does seem odd that she was so out of sorts.

Thomas Millar

Jeannie Ruddock Millar

William Ruddick Millar, aged 3

Thomas Millar Junior and William Ruddick Millar

Mary Millar, who raised the boys from 1912 onwards

William Millar

Jeannie Millar circa 1910

Ella Millar circa 1929

Jeannie Millar's grave in Victoria Cemetry, Carrickfergus,
which carries a dedication to Thomas Millar

The Titanic Engineers memorial in
Southampton, which includes Thomas Millar

Ruddick Millar, at the start of his writing career

Thomas Millar Junior, circa 1955

*Thomas Millar with the two pennies that he gave to Ruddick
before leaving Belfast on board Titanic on 2 April 1912*

The author at Belfast's Titanic Memorial with the two pennies given to her grandfather by his father as he boarded Titanic in 1912 - photo by Trevor Ferris

Descendants of the Millar children who met up at the family home in Boneybefore, summer 2010

Blue plaque unveiled in memory of Ruddick Millar on 8 February 2012, at the Millar home in Boneybefore - photo by Alan Lewis

Millar family members present at the unveiling of the plaque:
l-r: Herbie Calvert, Marcus Calvert, Fiona Hawkins, the author,
Lila Millar, Gillian Wicklow and Brian Wicklow

The wreaths on board MS Balmoral before they were laid at sea, during the memorial service held at 2:20am on Sunday 15 April 2012 - photo by Chris Helgren

The memorial service on the morning of 15 April 2012 at Titanic's final resting place

The author, on board MS Balmoral just after the
memorial service, 15 April 2012- photo by Chris Helgren

What Thomas Millar never got to see, The Statue of Liberty,
sailing into New York on Thursday 19 April 2012

Belfast's Titanic Memorial, restored in 2012 as part of the
Titanic Memorial Garden - photo by Gavin Moffitt

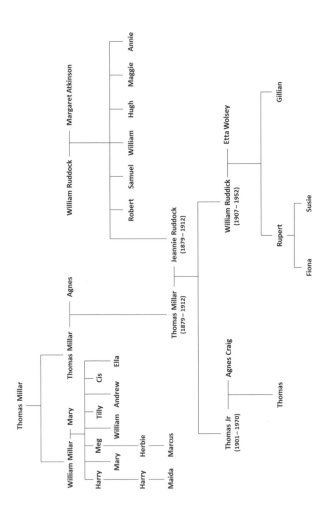

The Millar family tree

Chapter Twenty:

Ruddick Millar - January 1912

I knew something was wrong. People weren't acting the way they normally would.

Visitors came and went at all hours of the day and talked in hushed voices over cake and ginger wine. They looked at me as if I had done something wrong but was being forgiven for it. I wondered what it was I was supposed to have done.

Was it a holiday of some sort? It couldn't be Christmas because that was just over. Maybe it was Easter. You got eggs coloured with the dye from old neckties at Easter. Tommy and I were allowed to roll them down the street in the morning before church, or until we lost them which usually came first.

Or maybe it was the Twelfth. Folks did all sorts of funny things to celebrate the Twelfth of July in Belfast.

The little fat plumber from the next street, he would put a drum twice as fat as himself around his waist and beat it until the sweat ran down his red face and the blood dripped from his chubby hands.

All the while Mr McKinstry would toot on a small flute with little in the way of melody coming out of it. Then there were the banners with the pictures and strange titles. "Elijah and the Ravens", "Joseph and his Brothers", "The Secret of England's Greatness" and the rest. I can never work out what any of those things have to do with King Billy at the Boyne but they look good with all their rich colours fluttering in the breeze down Clifton Street.

I secretly was hoping that the Twelfth was the reason for all the callers to our house because Da had promised me that if I was very good for a few minutes at least I would be allowed to hold the string of one of the banners and there is no higher honour in the world than that.

It certainly didn't feel like a holiday.

Holidays were something meant for joy and laughter. Instead, people talked in low voices and went up and down the stairs slowly and silently with a kind of frown on their faces.

I even saw Aunt Maggie crying and she never cries about anything. No, it certainly wasn't a holiday. It was when Tommy came rushing into the yard screaming for his Ma that I decided to find out what was going on. If my brother wanted Ma then he would have to have her, even if she was upstairs in bed with a bad throat.

I was three stairs from the top when Uncle Bob stopped me. "Where are you away to?" he asked. "I'm going to see my Ma" I answered. "Tommy wants her.", "you can't see her", he said.

"Not even the night?" I asked because we were always allowed to kiss her goodnight even if she didn't feel well enough to get out of bed. She would always check we had said our prayers and say one more along with us.

"Not tonight or any other night," Uncle Bob said. "She's gone to heaven."

"I didn't see her go," I complained and went off to tell Tommy the news.

Next day, Tommy's classmates came to the house and past

Ma's bed with frightened faces. I was allowed to join them. For the first time in my life I felt funny inside but I couldn't speak or even cry like Aunt Maggie. When I saw Da and Uncle Bob and the rest of them carry a black box with shiny handles out into the street I knew that my Ma was inside and I would never see her again.

"Poor wee mite", I heard one of the neighbours say as they carried that box down the street. But I just held my head up high and tried my hardest not to cry because Da had always told me that men don't cry in front of other people.

There were certain things I could remember about my Ma, which I thought about every day after she was gone.

As time went on, I forgot little details about her like the way she wore her hair or the smell of her when she came to put me to bed at night, or the words of the songs she used to sing when we were going to sleep. I used to say my prayers at her knee every night. "God keep me tonight and forever, teach me to be brave and trust in thee."

That was our favourite, even though sometimes when I was saying the words I was thinking about my toy footballers, little alabaster men Uncle Hugh had given me, and how one of them had lost a leg, snapped off in an accident. If I could find it maybe Da could fix it back on for me.

Chapter Twenty-One:

Tom Millar - Early 1912

I took the coward's way out in the end. I had no idea how to tell my two lads their mother was dead and wouldn't be there for them anymore. So I didn't tell them. Not a word. Not anything at all. I figured they would stop asking eventually when she didn't come down from upstairs. What a stupid thing to do to my own children.

To think they would be so accepting. What kind of man am I that I can't even tell my own boys that their life has changed forever and they will live with heartache for a long, long time.

It all happened like a bad dream. I was working away in the engine sheds when I saw Hugh coming towards me. It's a rare sight for anyone who doesn't have a job in there to appear inside and come walking down the lines. I thought maybe something had happened to one of the boys and Jeannie had sent him down to tell me.

Instead of that, it was Annie who had sent him to find me. She had found Jeannie lying at the top of the stairs with hardly a breath in her body. She managed to get her onto the bed and sent for the doctor four streets away. By the time he got there, she was gone.

The doctor said she'd been carrying a bad infection for months now and it had weakened her heart.

The foreman let me go home but there was nothing to be

done apart from telling the rest of the family and starting to organise a funeral.

There was nothing I could do for her, my lovely strong, funny capable wife. I would really rather block all of this out rather than go over it again in my mind.

I have never felt pain like this and I don't know how to handle myself. I don't want to think about this at all. They say death is supposed to be a release, a peaceful slipping away into a better existence beyond. That's what people are trying to tell me in their words of comfort.

To me, it looked like someone had tapped my wife on the shoulder and told her she had to come with them to a place she wasn't ready to go. She was only 32. Ruddick is not even five years old.

Will he even remember his mother when he is a young man? Everyone round here has been very helpful, looking after the children, sending in food and just sitting with me a while. The neighbours have come over with pots of stew and soup to keep us fed. All the relatives have been round and we sit in the parlour with shades down and talk about what to do now for the best but nobody has come up with a magical plan which will stop me feeling like this and pave the way for the future.

The road ahead is very unclear. I can't think beyond the next tick of the big heavy clock which sits on our mantelpiece. The noise of it ticking is driving me to distraction. I never noticed it before. Now it shatters the silence, like life draining away.

I have to keep going to work to keep the money coming in, to keep a roof over our head but beyond that? I can't even think properly, no further than the next shift, the next meal, the next caller at the door.

Chapter Twenty-Two:

Maggie Ruddock - Early 1912

Since Jeannie died, I have been looking after my two nephews while their father is out at work. Nobody ever asked me if I would do it. Nobody said, "Maggie, do you mind stepping into your dead younger sister's shoes and bringing up her children for her?" I did it for the first week and everyone just assumed that would be my role from now on. Nobody thought maybe I wouldn't know how to talk to the wee bairns or whether I should tell them about their mother or not. I was just left to get on with it.

Of course, how could I have said no? My poor sister who was always so full of fun and life, I can't get used to the fact that she isn't around anymore. The least I can do for her is to make sure her boys have something to eat before they go out in the morning, have clean clothes on their backs and someone to soothe their cuts and bruises when they fall over.

Tommy the quiet one, he never opens his cheaper. Heaven only knows what is going on in that child's head. There is little chance of him sharing his thoughts with anyone. He is no trouble to look after but I worry about him because no child should be that quiet. He is out at school most of the day and I can't rightly say whether he is doing all right in his lessons or not because I have no idea where he is supposed

to be up to. I can only hope that if he is falling behind the masters will
tell me or his Da or someone.

Ruddick amuses himself until his brother gets home from
school, although he is a child of a thousand questions. I never met such
an inquisitive child.

When I am trying to get Tom's house tidied up and bread
baked for tea time, the wee child is constantly looking up at me with
his brown eyes and asking yet another question about something I
can't answer.

Not much of a word out of Tom, either. I don't expect him to
be full of chat just a few weeks after losing his wife but he has nothing
to say at all. It is like his mind is elsewhere and the events of this year
haven't been real to him. He came home from work yesterday without
even his coat on. He had left it down at the yard and walked all the way
home without even noticing how cold it was. The man is beside himself
with grief.

What I don't understand and what has caused all the talk
in our family is why he chose to bury her out at his home town in
Carrickfergus.

Sure, what connection has our Jeannie to there? She only ever
visited a couple of times. I know that's where Tom's people are from but
it's nothing to do with the Ruddocks.

I wouldn't have minded going to her grave from time to time
and maybe taking the children so that they don't forget about their
mother. I suppose I still could go but it's a fair trail all the way out
there. Even after you get off the train, it's still a good mile from the halt.
I haven't raised it with Tom because I doubt I would get an answer.

We didn't take the boys to the funeral. Maybe that was wrong,
but it was such a bitterly cold day.

I remember the day they put my mother in the ground and it isn't a memory I want to recall too often so I don't want to burden these two mites with the same thing.

Ruddick will be five soon. He is too young to be going to funerals and standing at gravesides. It's better they remember her the way she was when she was healthy and happy.

Memories like her lifting the mouth organ down from behind the china dog on the mantelpiece and making real melody from it. After the breakfast dishes were cleared away, she used to bring the family home to life with her music and songs. She brought such a smile to the boys' faces. Our Jeannie was always so full of life.

Now she's lying in a cold grave beside a stone wall in a seaside town twenty miles away where nobody knows her and nobody can come and visit her.

Chapter Twenty-Three:

Tommy Millar (Aged 11) - Early 1912

Nobody told me my Ma was dead. Not even Da.

Everything went quiet in our house. All you could hear all day long was the tick tock of the clock on the mantel. Then all these people started to call to our door and the kettle was always on the stove.

I thought Ma was up in bed not feeling well but then when she hadn't come down after a few days I thought maybe she didn't want to see anyone.

When my brother said that Uncle Bob had told him she was away to heaven, I thought he was making it up because sometimes Ruddick likes to make up stories in his head.

Then I saw Da and my uncles carrying a black box down the stairs and I knew it was true after all. And that's all I have to say about that.

Chapter Twenty-Four:

Tom Millar - March 1912

I got a letter a few weeks back, White Star want me to come and work for them.

They have offered me a job starting very soon as an assistant deck engineer. It looks like all those hours of study have been worth something after all. I have to do four or five trips as an assistant and then they move me up a grade.

Nearly £10 a month in wages, Jeannie would have loved that. That's a great wage to be sending home, enough to keep the boys and plenty for me to put by for the future, for our next home.

I have to do one voyage over to a place called Antwerp on a small ship, just to get a feel for it all. I need to know what is expected of me and who I will be taking orders from.

These ships are very big on a chain of command, like being in the forces.

Maggie is going to move in to my house full time when I am away. After that they will transfer me over to one of the big ships which crosses over the Atlantic to New York. There is a fair chance it could be the Olympic or even the Titanic.

Maggie said something about only looking after the boys in the short term. She says if I do go through with the plan of living in

America, we will have to think again.

I need to talk to Mary out in Carrick. She is more likely to take Tommy and Ruddick for a longer spell. Sure two more won't make much difference to her when she has eight of her own to feed as it stands. And she understands what it is like to suddenly lose your other half.

Chapter Twenty-Five:

Ruddick Millar - March 1912

Da says he is going away on a boat. Not the big boat he took us down to see at his work. Another one, a smaller one.

Maybe it is one you can see all at once and that really looks like a boat, not like the thing he was so proud of. Aunt Maggie is going to look after us until Da gets back.

I like Aunt Maggie because she lets me eat as many buns as I want after tea without telling me off and she doesn't scrub my neck hard when she is washing me.

Chapter Twenty-Six:

Mary Millar - March 1912

Tom's left his job at the Yard. Why would a man who has worked his way up and served his time walk out on a good steady job like that and take off into the unknown? I'll tell you why. Because the man is still grieving for his wife and he isn't thinking straight at all. Anyway he came out to see me with the boys to tell me about all these plans and how I fit into them.

When he comes back from Holland he's to turn around nearly right away and go on one of those big ocean liners across to America. He says he's going to get off there and live in New York. When he has found somewhere decent to live, got the lie of the land as he puts it, he is going to come and fetch the children over to be with him.

He says it is what Jeannie and he were planning before she died, that he would go out there and get everything set up for the rest of them to join him later. He says they had talked about it and decided it was the best thing to do for the boys' future. I never heard tell of this grand plan but then Tom has been so much of a stranger since William died.

I can't understand why he would want to take those two boys away to a strange country to live when all of their family are here in Ireland. Who is going to look after them when Tom is away on the boats?

I asked him all of these questions when he was out here on Sunday. I am not sure he answered any of the questions directly. He just is dead set on this plan and he can't see any other way but his. His mind is made up and there is no talking him out of it. He says all of the details will work themselves out when he gets there.

He says it is the best thing to give the children the best chance in life.

I felt like telling him that being born and raised in Boneybefore has never done any of my children any harm. I looked at those two boys standing in my house all dressed up in their Sunday collars and I thought to myself that they had had enough upheaval in the last three months without their dad sailing off for goodness knows how long.

I thought what would be best for them is to stay in the home they know after the shock of losing their mother so suddenly. What would be best for them is to stay right where they are until everybody has got a bit of sense back and is thinking straight again.

But when it comes down to it, they are not my children. They are Tom's. So I said none of that. If he is set on dragging them to the other side of the world where they know nobody then so be it, I can't sit here and tell him it might not be for the best.

While all this conversation was going on, young Ruddick took himself out to explore. He never stays in one place for too long, that one. He has a real problem standing still. Maybe a spell away in the country will do them both some good.

They can play on the beach, watch the trains go by, catch fish and play with their cousins.

Tommy, the older boy, he never left his father's side the whole time they were here visiting.

My Andrew tried to get him outside to kick a football around but he was having none of it. He is an odd one, Tom's eldest. It's like getting blood out of a stone to get any chat out of him whatsoever.

So the long and the short of it after that visit is that when Tom gets his instructions for the big voyage, the boys will come out here to stay for however long it takes.

They'll be sleeping up in the rafters with the rest of them, seven of them left since Harry moved out.

I don't even want to think where I will put them all. As usual, we will manage.

I could have insisted that some of Jeannie's family take them but in the end it is better that they are under a Millar roof.

Chapter Twenty-Seven:

Tom Millar - Late March 1912

I'm not sure how I feel. Proud, excited, nervous. Tomorrow I start work on Titanic. The very ship I watched growing up on the slipways for two years, and then the ship that I helped build the engines for is the one I will be working on going across the ocean.

Tomorrow I sign on and then the day after that we do our sea trials. Then we leave for Southampton and its goodbye to Ireland for a long while. I might never be back again. I have a clearer idea of what the job involves now and I know I can do it well. I have already met the fella who will be working immediately above me. He is a Belfast man too so that helps because we can talk to each other easily.

I have my little case packed up and ready to go. There is not much room in the place where us engineers will be staying on board so I haven't much with me. I don't need much. I hope Jeannie is proud of what I am doing. It is all done for her, not for me. I could easily have stayed on at the Yard but when this opportunity came up it was too good to turn my back on. I want all the things for my boys that I never got myself. I want for them all the opportunities in the world instead of being stuck here in Belfast where things don't feel right any more.

People are talking about Ireland breaking away from the rest of the country and some folk are getting worried about that. There is a lot of hatred in this city when you scratch the surface.

I have kept my last wage envelope from Harland's. There are a couple of coins I can give to the boys as a going away token for each of them. As well as that, there is a good bit to give Mary for looking after them. Annie is going to take them out there on the train after I have sailed. They can watch the big ship sailing down the Lough from Boneybefore.

I have asked them to wave their white handkerchiefs at me as Titanic passes but it will probably already be dark by then. I don't think Rudd has any idea how long it will be before I see him again. I think he reckons I am just going to work for a regular day like I normally do and I will be back in time for tea.

I've tried to tell him I will be gone until after the summer holidays but I don't think he has any grasp of how long that is. Anyway why would he believe anything I tell him after the way I handled his mother's death. I should have just told them outright instead of hiding it from them.

But how do you tell a small child with big brown eyes which would break your heart that the mother he adored isn't going to be around anymore?

Chapter Twenty-Eight:

Ruddick Millar - 2 April 1912

I like falling asleep underneath the thatch. I like the smell of the straw and the way it creaks at night time. Aunt Mary says it is cooling down after heating up in the sunshine all day long. This is where Tommy and I will be staying until Da gets back from his trip on the big boat. Tommy is going to a new school for a while.

He has to cross three fields to get there and one of the fields has cows in it. I wish I was going to school too. I have eight cousins here, so many I can't remember all of their names yet.

The nearest one to me in age is Ella. She didn't bother with me much when we first got here but yesterday she came and played with me at the little stream. Yesterday was the day my Da sailed away on his big boat. He is on board to help make it go. He brought Tommy and I down to the docks to say goodbye to him. I didn't want to see that big boat again but I knew this time he would be getting on to it and sailing away for a long time. I couldn't understand what all the people were cheering about because for me it was a sad day.

The big boat is taking my Da away on a big adventure. He says when he comes back he will have found a new place for the three of us to live. It will be in a different country from where we live now. I thought he had already found us a new place to live. I thought this was it.

All the time when he was waiting to get on board the big boat, my Da looked like he had something to say but didn't know how to begin.

He called Tommy and me over to one side, away from everyone else.

Then he pressed two shiny new pennies into both of our hands. I looked down at mine and wondered what he was doing. "They are this year's" he said. "Don't spend them until I see you again next." To Tommy he said, "Keep hold of them until I get back. I kept them out of my last wages specially for each of you." Then he told us to be good for Aunt Mary and not to play her up and to help out around the house. He ruffled my hair and then he was gone.

I think about him all of the time. It is strange not having him around. Last night I said a prayer for him like Ma had taught me. When I lay down to go to sleep beside Tommy I wondered where that big boat had been taking him to and where he is now.

Even though it was starting to get dark, Aunt Mary let us watch as the ship sailed past. She said it was a day to remember, a day that lots of people would look back on as the day the big ship, Titanic, left Belfast for the last time, left the place where it had been built.

My cousin, Harry said Da was on the boat and if I looked really hard I could see him. I strained my eyes as hard as I could and looked all over that boat but I couldn't see my Da anywhere. Maybe he was doing something on the inside to make smoke come out of the chimneys.

Whatever he was doing he didn't have time to stop and look out for me and Tommy in this little village by the sea.

We were standing on the wee beach on the other side of the

train tracks as big waves came in towards us. We both felt a bit strange. Even Tommy said so because now we are living here with people we don't know very well.

There were three wee boats with Titanic. Harry said they were showing it the way to go from the Lough out into the wide open sea. If the big boat can't find her own way out of Belfast, how will it find the way to all the faraway places? I wonder how long it will be before my Da comes back again?

Maybe he will have changed his mind and we will all go back to Hillman Street to live and everything will go back to the way it was before.

Chapter Twenty-Nine:

Mary Millar - 10 April 1912

I'm a bit long in the tooth to be looking after a five year old. It's lucky the boy seems to be able to amuse himself in his own little world. I couldn't have him running underneath my feet when I am trying to get everything done for the rest of them. I haven't time to be entertaining a wee boy.

Tom left me enough money to keep the pair of them for a couple of months. He says he'll send more when he gets his first pay. He said by the summer he should have himself sorted out with a place to live and if Harry can bring them as far as Southampton, he can take them the rest of the way. I still don't the he has thought it all through, I mean who is going to look after them out there where they don't know anyone? He keeps saying it will all fall into place.

That's always been Tom, he is one of those people who always lands on his feet no matter how little planning he puts into the whole thing.

If William had come up with a scheme like that when he was alive, I doubt anyone would have been willing to go along with looking after our children for who knows how long. Tom always had that knack of getting people around to his way of thinking. Before you realise, you've agreed to do whatever he asked and that's all settled and it's too late to back out.

The older one hasn't come out of himself at all. Don't get me wrong, I have no problem with a quiet child but Tommy looks lost all the time. The younger ones have tried to take him under their wings but he is a lost cause. He must be feeling the loss of his mother more than Ruddick because he understands better what has happened.

Half the time I think Ruddick reckons his mother has gone away somewhere for a while and she will be back any time now. Poor child, I don't think he understands what all has happened to him since the start of the year.

Ella has adopted Ruddick like a new puppy. She thinks he is there as her playmate. She has started to try to make him join in all sorts of girl games with her. I doubt that will last much longer before he puts his foot down and goes back to fishing in the sea with Andrew.

Chapter Thirty:

Tom Millar - 10 April 1912

We have been in Southampton nearly a week now, waiting to go. The passengers started to board the ship this morning and there was fierce excitement. Trains were arriving down from London with all the fine ladies and gentlemen and all their servants running after them and carrying their bags. Huge amounts of bags and trunks. What could they have in all that luggage?

More stuff crammed into trunks than Jeannie and I had ever owned between us. All the time I have known this ship I only ever thought of it as steel and engines. It is only now that passengers are starting to get on board to go on their journeys that she becomes real, more than something we built at Queens Island.

I watched this ship grow over three years in Belfast. Now she is more than a piece of engineering, she is floating palace. Of course us engineers don't get to see much beyond our own quarters and where we work.

But on the way over from Belfast when there were just a few dozen crew on board, we had a good look round at the first and second class quarters and where they will take their meals.

There is even a Turkish bath on this thing. Me and this other fella, one of the young apprentices who got a place on the Guarantee group with Mr Andrews, we walked the length of the ship through the salons, the smoking rooms, the reading rooms.

We could do that a few days ago but not now. Now we know our place, down in the engineers quarters, never seen, never heard. No salons for us, no gymnasium. Maybe if I make enough money in America, I can afford to travel in style like this. I can't see the Millars ever travelling in first class but perhaps we can work our way up the ladder a little further.

From Southampton we go across the English Channel to France where we pick up more passengers and cargo. Then would you believe it, it's back to Ireland.

We stop at Queenstown, the last land we will see until we get to the other side of the ocean. By the time everyone has boarded there will be more than two thousand people on board this ship.

There is plenty of room for everyone too. There was me thinking I wouldn't see Irish soil again for many a month and as it turns out, a few days after leaving I am back there again, at the other end of the country. I won't actually touch land, though.

They bring the passengers out to us on a tender ship because the wharf isn't big enough to take ships this size. It's the same in France, which is a shame because I can't say that I set foot in the country, not this time around anyway.

When I wasn't on duty this morning I took up carving the little men again. It gives me something to do rather than going ashore or just staring into space and thinking. I can send the men back home or wait and give them to the boys in person.

Tommy is getting a bit big for toy figures now so I have tried to make them look like soldiers.

I am sure they are all right with Mary. She will keep them in line and they have plenty of cousins to play with. It will be good for them to live in the countryside for a while, so much better than the smoky city air. They can do all the things I used to do when I was a boy growing up there.

I miss the two of them though. I have to keep remembering that I am doing this for their welfare.

I started to write a letter to them but I didn't get too far. I have never been much of a letter writer. It's too hard to know what to say.

Chapter Thirty-One:

Tommy Millar - April 1912

It is very noisy here. There are so many people living in one small house, there is no space to take yourself away from everyone. Andrew is trying to be my friend and that's all right but my friends are back in Belfast, not out here in the country.

Maybe when Da gets to America, he won't like it after all and we can go back to our own house in Hillman Street.

This is a funny wee house we are living in now. It doesn't have a proper upstairs or a proper kitchen and there aren't enough rooms for everybody.

Hillman Street had two lots of upstairs and plenty of places where you could go and hide or be on your own for a bit.

Aunt Mary says it means there aren't so many stairs to climb but I can't see that climbing stairs is any hardship.

At night time I can hear the owls hooting and the waves breaking on the beach across the road. They all told me I have to be careful crossing over the railway line in case I get hit by a train.

They don't realise I am used to looking after myself in town. They treat me like a wee boy. Even if you didn't see the train coming towards you, and you can see it coming down the track for miles in each direction, how could you not hear it coming and smell the smoke and hear the driver sounding the whistle?

They must think I am as thick as two short planks if I can't cross a railway track without getting run over by a railway engine.

I do try to be nice to them and to talk to my cousins and answer all their questions about what it's like to live up in Belfast but the older ones like Matilda give me such pitying looks that it is hard not to feel like an outsider.

I hope Da comes back soon and tells us all it was a big mistake and things will go back to how they were last summer.

Chapter Thirty-Two:

Mary Millar - 17 April 1912

I don't know what to tell the children. Nobody can quite believe what has happened.

That big ship, the one all those men put so much work into, it only left two weeks ago and now it's at the bottom of the ocean and all those people with it. What chills my heart is what has happened to Tom. The newspapers said everyone was saved. That was the first news we got and we were just waiting to hear from Tom or from his employers. The papers said everyone was picked up by another boat before Titanic sank and that they were all taken to New York. Now they are saying that more people drowned than were saved. People are starting to say that hundreds of folk have been lost at sea.

The newspapers are saying that when the rescue ship pulled in to harbour in America, most of the passengers from Titanic were missing. If they didn't get all the passengers off, what hope is there for the crew?

I dread the news that will come next. It is best not to mention it to the children until I know for sure what has happened. Perhaps Tom will get in touch soon, send us a letter to let us know he is safe. I will wait for that letter to arrive.

Chapter Thirty-Three:

Tommy Millar - 18 April 1912

At school today, the headmaster called everyone together in the big main room because he wanted to talk to us.

We all thought we had done something wrong and would have to get extra work or stay behind after lessons had finished. Nobody could work out what it was we were supposed to have done that was bad. But it wasn't that at all.

The master said he had some important news to tell us about something awful that had happened in the world. He said a big ship carrying some of the most important people in the world had sunk in the middle of the Atlantic Ocean and that a lot of people had been drowned.

He said it was a very sad thing for all of those people but also for us here in Ireland because the ship had been built in Belfast. Then he said the name of the ship.

It was Titanic and that is the same name as the ship my Da sailed on, going to America.

I didn't say anything to the master or any of the others because I am sure he has made a mistake. My Da wouldn't build a ship that would sink on its first voyage.

He would build a proper ship that would float no matter what it crashed into. Sure when I saw that ship it was the biggest thing ever built, they said.

So how could it sink after hitting a lump of ice? It can't be right. The master must have made a mistake. I am sure my Da will be coming back any day now and sending for us.

Chapter Thirty-Four:

Ella Millar - Early May 1912

Today when I finished gathering the eggs, I came back into the house to find Ma crying.

She was sitting in the chair by the fire just staring straight ahead while big tears ran down her wrinkled face. Ma never cries. Cis said she saw her cry once when we visited Da's grave in town but I don't remember that at all.

Ma had got a letter. A man on a bicycle brought it this morning. Ma stuffed it into her apron pocket and said she would deal with it later. Whatever was written in that letter had made her cry. I wondered what could be such sad news.

When she saw me looking at her and watching her crying, she put her handkerchief up to her eyes, folded up a piece of paper and got up, trying to pretend that everything was all right. But I knew that it wasn't and even when I asked her she told me to go and play.

I know that a few weeks back she sat down at the big table and wrote a long letter to someone. It took her ages to write it and she kept starting over. Ma doesn't write to anybody so I don't know who it was to. When I asked her she said it was a very important letter and she couldn't tell me what it was about just now. So I asked her if the letter that had made her cry was from the person she had written to, the important person. She didn't answer but by the look on her face I could tell that I was right.

Later I found that letter and I knew it was wrong for me to read it but I looked at it anyway just in case it meant we were going to get sent away or couldn't afford the rent on the house or something bad like that. I read some of the words on the page.

It was talking about Uncle Tom. It said he was "lost." What could that mean? How could you get lost when you are on a boat going to a place across the sea?

Did it mean the ship had lost its way? Or was he lost on board the ship. Surely someone would be able to find him if they looked everywhere and searched from top to bottom?

Or did he get to America and get lost there. I remember we went up to Belfast one day on the train and Ma got lost for a few minutes because she said everything had changed.

Maybe that is what happened to Uncle Tom. He got confused when he got off the boat and couldn't find where he was supposed to be staying.

Ma tells us if we get lost when we are out playing in the fields and we can't see over the top of the tall grass that we have to look for the sea. "Remember you live beside the sea", she used to say. "Find your way back to the shore and you will be all right. But don't stray too far away". Uncle Tom must have strayed too far away. He should look for the sea and then he can find his way.

Before I went to bed I asked Ma if Uncle Tom was lost and where he had got lost.

She sighed heavily and she must have been lost in thought because she didn't think to scold me for looking at the letter which I shouldn't have done. "Your Uncle Tom was on that big boat which sank," she said.

"It means he won't be home. He was drowned. The people he worked for let me know. I haven't told the boys yet. I haven't told anyone so don't you go saying to Ruddick or Tommy, especially not wee Ruddick. He is too young to understand".

I said I wouldn't say to anyone but that will be difficult because when my Da died, I was only two and I don't really remember but I would have liked to have been told right away. All this keeping secrets from people or just not telling them because you don't want them to be hurt is not a good thing I think.

Chapter Thirty-Five:

Ruddick Millar - Early May 1912

Today started off like any other day. It was quite warm, not raining and the sun was shining a little.

I have a lot of different games I like to play when everyone else is at school. I will get to go to school next year, Aunt Mary says. The best game is to stand knee deep in the water and spear sticklebacks and razor fish as they go from the stream into the sea. It takes a lot of patience and when I first started to do it, I hardly speared any. But with practice, I have got quite good at it and now I can catch more than Andrew. We stand for hours fishing for the wee stick insects and then count up at the end who has the most.

We also look for cockabillions on the sand flats when the tide is out. Another game I like to play by myself is to sail paper boats on the burn that runs through the centre of the village. It runs right downhill by the lane.

Matilda says one family owns the land on one side and another family owns the fields and houses on the other side.

Anyway my brother Tommy taught me how to make little paper boats out of the pages of an exercise book. He folds it over and over again and before you know it, you have a little paper boat that you can sail on the water.

I tried putting one of my wooden men inside but he was too heavy. I am not as quick at making the boats as Tommy is and sometimes I get it wrong so it is easier to ask him to make them for me.

So today I decided that is what I would do, to see if I could get one of the boats to sail all the way down the stream without stopping. I could follow it by running along on the bank.

I managed to get it about half way down and then I realised that school must have been finished because I could see Ella coming up the lane. She started to come towards me but then she stopped for a moment as if unsure whether to come ahead. I waved at her. I like Ella because she isn't like the other girls who play with dolls and stupid things. Ella likes to climb trees and paddle in the sea with me. As she came closer to me I could see there was a worried almost frightened look on her face. She seemed uneasy. She was looking at my paper boat in the stream.

While I had taken my eyes off it for a second, the paper craft had sailed downstream, hit a rock in the middle of the river, filled with water, quivered and then sunk into the stream.

I watched as some of the terror faded from Ella's eyes. "So your wee boat's sunk," she observed. I nodded my head and gazed at my late liner now returned to its original form of an exercise book page.

"Do you remember the big boat your Da sailed away on?" she asked.

How could I forget it. Sometimes I dreamed that the big boat had turned around as soon as it was out of sight and sailed right back to Belfast again.

"It went just like your wee boat", she said. "It hit an iceberg. A lot of people drowned. Your Da was drowned too."

It took me a moment or two to understand what she had told me. "Then will my Da be home?" I asked her. "No", she said. "Not ever".

My thoughts immediately turned to the gold watch my Da used to wear in his top pocket. Such a lovely one, it always fascinated me. It was so shiny I swear it must have been worth a lot of money. What a pity if it was lost along with my Da. "And his gold watch too?" I asked Ella. "Yes, she replied, "everything is gone."

I stared downstream again unable to take in what she was telling me. Da gone too? To the same place as Ma? A place where I would never see them again?

"Come on home," Ella said. "Tommy will make you another wee boat."

"No," I said. "I hate boats, I don't want anything more to do with boats."

Chapter Thirty-Six:

Ruddick Millar (Aged 27) - 1934

I swore I would never get on a ship. I swore it would be the very last thing I would do. Considering what happened to our family over twenty years ago now, I said on that basis I was done with boats forever, and I meant it. And yet, here I stand at the harbourside preparing to board a steamer which will meet a train to take me to London, all in the furtherance of my own career. History repeats itself. My father boarded a ship to further his career and to improve the prospects for my brother and me. It ended in disaster.

Let's hope I have more luck with my small enterprise, miniscule when compared to the scale of his adventure in 1912. So much for sticking to my guns. I am preparing for my first ever boat journey because I have no alternative. There is a stretch of water between me and London and on the map is doesn't look negotiable by swimming!

So despite all my childish protestations I am abandoning my principles and putting my fate in the hands of the sea, for a few hours at least in search of literary fame and fortune.

22 years ago my 33 year old father perished in the cold Atlantic, leaving my brother and me in the care of an Aunt. His plan had been to work his passage on Titanic as an engineer and then to

send for us when he had found us a new home in New York. That was
the plan. The reality was somewhat different.

A great, big iceberg in the middle of the ocean stood in the
ship's path and it had other ideas about our destiny. I often wonder
how things would have turned out for us all if Titanic had not hit
that iceberg, or if my father had found a path to safety on that night. I
dread to think what his final hours must have been like, thinking of his
children I am sure and cursing himself for his bold adventure stopped
cruelly in its tracks.

I remember receiving that terrible news. I remember how I
went back to the cottage in Boneybefore after my cousin Isabella had
imparted the news in the softest way she could think of, and how I
clutched into my hand the two penny pieces my father had given me
before he sailed with the words, "Don't spend those until I see you
again." I remember how I clutched them so tightly in my grief that the
date of 1912 was almost burnt into my palm like a brand.

Just as that date was impressed into my hand, so too was the
day stamped on my memory. It became a watershed, a turning point
for me and my older brother, a realisation that despite the family
around us, we were alone in the world.

I was too young to understand what had happened, how I had
found myself an orphan within the space of three short months.
My poor aunt, not a young woman, was entrusted with our care for a
matter of months. Instead she became a somewhat unwilling substitute
mother to two extra sons until they were grown. She brought us up,
clothed and fed us and made sure we paid attention to our lessons. It
wasn't what she had agreed to do for my father but she was left with
no choice than to finish the job and, to her credit, we were unaware of
being treated any differently to the rest of her brood.

She received a meager weekly donation from the Titanic Fund. I found out just recently that our subsistence came from benefactors, not from my father's employers or those who had built the ship which sank. It was a hand out from wealthy folk with a conscience for the poor little Irish children left penniless by the Titanic disaster. I am sure those weekly pay outs, although seen as charity, were a welcome addition to Mary Millar's family pot.

We lived on in that funny cottage in Boneybefore until I was 12 years old. By then, two of my female cousins were training as schoolmistresses and to find work, it was necessary to move up to the city.

Cis and Matilda found us a three storey house in Atlantic Avenue. The irony of the name was not lost on me. The Atlantic Ocean had claimed my father's life, and here I was moving to a street which glorified its name.

The day we moved from Boneybefore was a comical event. Our furniture, such as it was, was stacked up aboard a cart driven by two men and a horse. The drivers had more interest in the roadhouses along the route than the safe transport and delivery of the Millar family belongings we had carefully packed up. The driver and his helper must have been thirsty on that warm summer's day because they felt it necessary to stop at every roadhouse between Carrick and Belfast to quench their thirst.

I, of course, was left outside to look after the contents of the cart and the restless horse. It was an incredibly long journey. It is from that house in Atlantic Avenue that I have set out today for the next stage of my life's adventure. Our family settled well there, even though it was a stark contrast to the tumbledown thatch of Boneybefore. My cousin, Harry stayed in the village with his own young family so we were not saying goodbye forever to the little hamlet which hugged the shore near Kilroot train halt. I used to stay with Harry and his children in the long summer holidays when the time from dinner to tea seemed an eternity, and one Christmas to the next was a vast chasm of time. Up in the city, I was sent to the local school run by the Baptists and affectionately known as "The Bap". I have my school records to this day in a volume labelled "Judgement Book".

My every misdemeanour, my progress in reading and writing and my growing interest in books and composition is all charted in those pages. My late arrival due to some distraction or other along the route, which had fired my imagination in a different direction, all is recorded on these yellowing pages. A master there, a W.P. Brown, took a particular interest in my academic career.

He called me into his study one day to tell me that, as a Titanic orphan, I had been awarded a special type of scholarship, which would take care of my books, tuition and so forth. It was a relief to my aunt who would rather I had gone out to work at an early age. I though little of the gesture at the time but upon making enquiries years later, it became apparent that no such fund existed. This kindly man had been paying for me from his own pocket and fearful that should be offended by the idea of charity, he had disguised it as my rightful grant. I am forever grateful to W.P. Brown for his kindness,

Before I took the train to Larne this morning, passing by my former home in Boneybefore, I went for a final look around the city. I wanted to take a walk around the City Hall and to say silent goodbyes to Belfast. The tram terminated at Castle Junction and I walked the short distance along Donegall Place towards Queen Victoria's statue. As I walked, my mission became clear.

My editor had asked me for a few lines of prose as a prologue to the book he had agreed to publish, the second such volume which has been successful in reaching printed form. I have been at a loss as to what to write. He wants me to give me reader an idea of how I have got to this point in my career at what he sees as a tender age.

How have I become a renowned author, playwright, journalist, held in high regard by the literary circle in our small city?

The phrase "next big thing" has been attached to my name. But to sum up this successful rise to stardom from humble beginnings is an objective task which I feel ill-qualified to undertake. I hoped to find my inspiration under the dome of Belfast's magnificent civic building but as I walked towards Donegall Square, my footsteps turned in a different direction, towards the Titanic Memorial upon which my father's name is engraved.

The tragedy of the Titanic was undoubtedly overtaken in scale by the terrible losses at the Battle of the Somme four years later. That event has eclipsed the loss of the great liner, Titanic in the minds of most Ulster people. The memorial itself, suffering the effects of city soot and grime after just fourteen years in position, is a testament to how forgotten the disaster has become.

The Yard has moved on, Belfast has moved on. The event is rarely spoken of, certainly since the creation of this new state of Northern Ireland.

As I look at my father's name, Thomas Millar, fourth from the top of the list of is White Star colleagues, I realised that I must move on too. I must cut the ties. My mother's memorial is in my own heart and engraved on a mossy headstone in Carrick which I seldom visit. I have lost contact with the Ruddock side of the family, her multitude of good natured siblings.

Even my own brother and I are no longer in regular contact.

We were never close despite our hard start to life. I realize it is time for me to set off on a new course, even if it means crossing a small stretch of sea to do so.

As I step onto the steamer in the fading light, I reach into my breast pocket, there, rolled up in a handkerchief are the two pennies, as shiny as the day they were minted and as shiny as the day they were handed to me by my father as a token of his affection.

Epilogue

Ruddick Millar had a successful career as a journalist, author and playwright.His time in London was not so successful and he returned after a matter of months.

He married Etta Wolsey and had two children, Rupert in 1935 and Gillian in 1944. He died in 1952 at the age of 46 from a heart attack. Two years previously he had received a payment from the National Disasters Relief Fund. The £200 cheque was in "full and final settlement" of his claim.

He had five granddaughters, none of whom he lived to know. Four of them now live in England, one remains in Belfast working in journalism and in the burgeoning Titanic industry.

Tommy Millar married and brought up a family in North Belfast. He had at least one son, also called Thomas. The brothers kept in touch but were not close, possibly because of the six year age difference. Tommy did not keep the two pennies his father gave him before boarding Titanic. He and his son attended Ruddick's funeral but the families lost touch afterwards.

Of the eight Millar children from Boneybefore, three had children of their own. The descendants of Meg Millar Calvert, Harry Millar and their cousin, Ruddick met up at the cottage in Boneybefore in the summer of 2010.

On February 8 2012, a blue plaque was unveiled at the Millar family cottage in Boneybefore, near Carrickfergus, County Antrim to commemorate Ruddick Millar's life and work.

The Titanic Memorial Cruise

April 2012

In 2008, I was contacted by a travel agency in the West of England about taking part in a cruise ship voyage which would retrace Titanic's route across the North Atlantic and mirror the exact dates. At first I didn't know what to think. It seemed like a great idea but I had never been on a cruise ship before and was worried about being tied to a schedule. I also wasn't sure where I wanted to be on 15th April 2012. There was a yearning to be with family in my home city on such an important date.

I was offered the chance to perform lectures on board and therefore work my passage. The more I thought about it, the more I realised the advantages of taking part in such a voyage. It would allow me to visit the site where Titanic spent her last hours and to pay tribute to my great grandfather, Thomas Millar who was lost in the Titanic disaster. And as well as that, it would allow me to complete the journey he didn't get to finish in 1912. My husband Gavin and I decided we would go.

Four years were not long in going by, during which time I was building my business as a Titanic tour guide, lecturer and author. On Friday 6th April, Good Friday, I found myself boarding the MS Balmoral in Belfast as it finished of a mini cruise around the significant

Titanic ports in the UK. The opportunity to make an early entrance
to the Titanic Memorial cruise meant I could recreate my great
grandfather's exact journey. My husband had a couple more days of
work so he was to join us in Cobh the following Monday.

As we sailed down Belfast Lough, I made a point of standing
out on deck until we had passed Whitehead and the Copeland Islands.
I wanted to be able to see the village of Boneybefore, just outside
Carrickfergus. It was from here that my 5 year old grandfather watched
Titanic sail out of Belfast Lough on the evening of April 2nd. His father
was on board and he described how he couldn't understand why all the
other people watching Titanic's departure were cheering and waving
as he felt so sad to witness his father sailing away. I wanted to mirror
that moment by marking the moment of passing Boneybefore from
my great grandfather's point of view. Any sad thoughts I may have had
were headed off by the goodwill text messages I was receiving from
friends on both sides of the Lough as they watched Balmoral sail past.

When we left Southampton a few days later, there was a
small crowd to see us off but nothing of substance. It was all the more
surprising then, when we arrived in Cobh on Monday evening to see
the hillsides and streets lined with thousands of people to wish us well.
There was a civic reception and we were made to feel extremely special
by the welcome extended by the people of Cobh. First time visitors to
Ireland were genuinely touched to see such a turnout.

My own time on board Balmoral was spent listening to my
fellow lectures, preparing for my own talks and working for the
BBC crew who were on board to broadcast live from the ship. It was
a pleasure to be in the company of Titanic luminaries such as Jack
Eaton and Charlie Haas. These two men have spent years of their lives
researching details of the Titanic story and yet they made me feel that

I had as much to contribute to the story as anyone else in the lecturing pool. I will not forget Charlie's kindness in making me feel that I had a valuable contribution to make.

Media coverage of the Titanic memorial cruise may have suggested that it was one big floating party. This would not be an accurate representation of the atmosphere on board. While people had gone to a lot of trouble to wear 1912 costumes, this was as a tribute and celebration to the great age of steam liners. There was no suggestion that this was in any way disrespectful to the loss of 1500 lives and I never for a moment found anything to be inappropriate or of questionable taste.

As we approached the wreck site on the evening of Saturday 14th April, I could sense a change in atmosphere. The ship was quieter, people were in a reflective mood and when the three wreaths which were to be thrown into the ocean were put on display in the main theatre, it started to come home to all of us that we were there for a very important reason and were about to be part of a significant remembrance of an important and poignant historical moment.

We had experienced some quite rough weather on our journey to mid Atlantic but as we approached the wreck site, conditions changed. It became incredibly calm, like a millpond. The sky was clear and one planet shone so brightly that its light was reflected in the water. Writing about Titanic in 1934, my grandfather had described it as a "calm, star-crowned night." History was repeating itself. Gavin was following our progress on his GPS and as the engines slowed down, he turned to me and said, "we're here." To think that the vast hull of Titanic lay underneath the water was an awesome feeling. Here, in the middle of nowhere, where no other lights shone, was the place where Titanic had met her fate and where my great grandfather had spent his last hours, no doubt thinking of the two sons who were to be left orphaned by his attempts to get them a better start in life in America.

The commemoration took the form of two services, one indoors and the other on the deck at the stern of the ship. There were about 22 families of Titanic passengers and crew represented on the cruise and we were given a privileged position at the front of the crowds. The ship's whistle was sounded at the moment when Titanic would have hit the iceberg and again to mark 2.20am, when she sank beneath the surface of the water. What will stay with me forever is how quickly that time passed. When played out in real time, you realise just how little time there was for people to be put into lifeboats. If anything, it was an incredible feat to get 700 people off the ship. The moment when the wreaths were thrown into the ocean was the point at which I finally felt the emotion of loss for my great grandfather. I could imagine what it must have been like for him so far from home in the last moments of his life.

Many of my fellow passengers chose to stay up for the entire night and to watch the dawn break in the same way as lifeboat passengers would have waited for rescue to appear. There was a shared sense that we had taken part in something incredibly special and we had been privileged to be part of an event which had paid a fitting tribute to the 1500 souls lost on that April night exactly one hundred years ago.

As I said earlier, my whole reasoning for taking part in the crossing was to complete the journey into New York for my great grandfather so four days later, we were set to arrive in New York City, early in the morning. We got up at 5am in order to get a good spot from where we could see the Statue of Liberty and the skyline of Manhattan. As we sailed down the coast of Long Island, the green and red buoys marking the channel sounded their lonely bells as they bobbed in our wake. It was truly haunting, as if sounding a death knell for the lost passengers and crew of Titanic. Beside us were new friends we had made, Gwyn and Tim, a Canadian couple with whom we had enjoyed dinner on several occasions during the cruise and with whom I hope we remain in touch. In the distance, we could make out the shape of One World Trade Center, the new skyscraper built near the site of the Twin Towers. The parallel has to be drawn between over three thousand deaths in 9/11 and the Titanic disaster which claimed half of that number. We felt it only fitting during our visit to New York to pay tribute to those victims as part of our journey.

There was no obvious welcoming party in New York which I found a little disappointing. Considering the significance of what we had just done, I had expected perhaps a few small vessels would come out to greet us, but New York is a tough city with business to get on with and no such flotilla guided us in.

I will never forget my two weeks at sea on board Balmoral, the friends I made and the experiences we shared. If Tommy Millar is looking down, I hope he approves of the tribute his great granddaughter paid to him on behalf of the rest of the Millar family, the people of Belfast and of Northern Ireland.